Bilbao

everest

Editorial management: Raquel López Varela

Editorial coordination: Aizkorri argitaletxea

Text: Xabi Larrañaga Muñoz

Photographs: Santiago Yániz, Mikel Alonso y Archivo Everest

Photographs of the Guggenheim Museum: Mikel Alonso y Santiago Yániz
© FMGB Guggenheim Bilbao Museoa

Diagrams: Luis Alonso

Cover design: Francisco A. Morais

Digital images processing: David Aller

Cartography: © Everest

Translated by: EURO:TEXT

Editorial Everest would like to thank you for purchasing this book. It has been created by an extensive and complete publishing team made up of photographers, illustrators and authors specialized in the field of tourism, together with our modern cartography department. Everest guarantees that the contents of this work were completely up to date at the time of going to press, and we would like to invite you to send us any information that helps us to improve our publications, so that we may always offer QUALITY TOURISM.

Please send your comments to:
Editorial Everest. Dpto. de Turismo
Apartado 339 – 24080 León (Spain)
Or e-mail them to us at turismo@everest.es

© EDITORIAL EVEREST, S. A.
Carretera León-La Coruña, km 5 - LEÓN
ISBN: 978-84-441-3238-9
Depósito legal: LE. 618-2012
Printed in Spain

EDITORIAL EVERGRÁFICAS, S. L.
Carretera León-La Coruña, km 5
LEÓN (España)

"The whole world is a bigger Bilbao." (Miguel de Unamuno)

Classic view of 18th century Bilbao, as depicted
in a 1784 drawing by Thomas Morony.

THE OLD BILBAO – EL VIEJO BILBAO

The official history of Bilbao started more than seven centuries ago, on 15th June, 1300. Diego López de Haro, Lord of Vizcaya, signed Bilbao's Town Charter in Valladolid. The very small population was, at that time, distributed along both banks of the Estuary. The left bank, known today as Bilbao La Vieja (Old Bilbao), was where miners and their families lived. Diego López de Haro chose the right bank, inhabited by a few fishermen, to establish the new town. Three streets, Somera, Artecalle and Tendería, formed the first urban nucleus which could be accessed through two gates: Atxuri, which faced Durango and Balmaseda and Zamudio, which faced the Asúa Valley. One century later, the bilbaínos (the people of Bilbao), of whom there were fewer than two thousand, took charge of the building project for the church of Santiago, which is now a cathedral. By that time, rapid economic and demographic growth of the area was the reason for further expansion to include four new

Above, a postcard showing El Arenal Bridge in 1878.
Below, the Church of San Antón and the adjacent bridge, from a 19th century engraving by J. E. Delmas.

streets: Belosticalle, Carnicería Vieja, Barrencalle and Barrencalle Barrena. This was how the so-called Siete Calles (Seven Streets) came into being, the core of what is now called the **Casco Viejo (Old Quarter)**.

THE OLD QUARTER

The Old Quarter is the sum of these Seven Streets and those which followed in the direction of **El Arenal**. The catastrophic floods of 1983, when the water level rose various metres, meant that it had to be renovated. It boasts more than 800 shops and 200 bars and restaurants. The best way to see it is starting from the **Puente de San Antón** which joins both banks of the Estuary. This bridge used to be the entrance point for Castilian wool and the exit point for

Panoramic view of Bilbao's Old Quarter.

This page, two views of La Ribera Market. Right, a stained glass window featuring the city's coat of arms; below, a wiew of the market built around 1920 on the site of the port's first quays.

for presiding over public events which were held in the **plaza Vieja**, located in the area which today accommodates the **Mercado de La Ribera**. Built in the early 20 th century, it is claimed to be Europe's largest indoor market. In 2010, following the discovery of severe structural damage, it was almost completely demolished and rebuilt. The fish, meat and fruit and vegetable stalls provide a keen insight into the superb quality of Basque cuisine. The market occasionally hosts cultural events, fashion shows and theatre. It is known by locals as 'La Plaza'.

*Above, a view of Calle de la Cruz in the Old Quarter.
Left, the popular Café Bilbao, in Plaza Nueva.*

The Old Quarter can be accessed via Calle Ronda, n.º 16 of this street was the birthplace of the writer Miguel de Unamuno. Ronda was originally outside the urban heart. It was from here that the entrance to the town was guarded and remains of the wall can still be seen today in the alley Cantón de Camarón. Calle Somera, characterised by high buildings due to the scarcity of land for building, can be reached via this alley.

The passage of history and, in particular, the bombardments during the second Carlista War, have erased almost all medieval remnants. This is a typical area for having tapas and drinks in various bars which is referred to as tapeo and chiquiteo respectively, a very popular custom amongst the bilbaínos. Alongside door number 12 is a plaque indicating this as the birthplace of the musician Juan Crisóstomo de Arriaga.

Next page, Bidebarrieta street.

*Previous page,
the Cathedral's
Neo-Gothic
façade and tower.*

The Cathedral's Gothic cloister.

*Concelebration of a mass to mark the reopening of the Cathedral
for public worship following exhaustive restoration work.*

Exterior of the Church of Los Santos Juanes.

Tendería is reached by crossing Artecalle via Cantón Alejandro de la Sota. This is where the **church of Santiago** is located. It was awarded the status of **cathedral** in 1950 and represents the most important religious building in Bilbao. From the start of its construction, in 1379, it has been a key stop along The Coastal Section of the Pilgrim's Route to Santiago. Its tremendous portico was started in 1571 and was, at the same time, used as a buttress, cemetery and covered market. The interior with its three naves is worth a visit, the ambulatory and the triforium are outstanding. The main doorway is the work of Severino de Achúcarro, neogothic in style, and looks onto a small square dominated by the baroque **fountain of Santiago**, designed in 1785 by the artist Luis Paret. Those visiting the city during a public holiday may be lucky enough to witness the enthralling *aurresku*, a dance to greet visitors that is very popular at Basque weddings. During the August festival, large crowds of locals gather in the square in the early evening to enjoy the traditional dances. At one side of the cathedral, on the **puerta del Ángel** (The Angel's Door) from 1515, a pilgrim's shell can be observed, emphasising how significant Bilbao has been for The Way of St. James. It is not in vain that the Apostle St. James the Elder has been Patron Saint of the town since 1643.

The **portal de Zamudio** (Gate of Zamudio) is a few steps away and was the entrance for rural products to the town. In days gone by, this entrance was defended by a tower which was later converted into a prison. The nearby **Santos Juanes** church possesses remarkable baroque altarpieces. The Jesuits had rooms at the rear which stood round a cloister with three floors. Today it houses the **Basque Museum**, which can be accessed via Plaza de Unamuno. It is constantly undergoing a process of renovation,

The mausoleum of the powerful Bilbao family, the Arana-Varonas, situated inside the Cathedral.

The Basque Museum. The Cloister and «Mikeldi», an enigmatic protohistoric idol.

however one of the objects always worth visiting is the Mikeldi, the stone block in the shape of a pig or wild boar, elaborated during the Iron Age. It has a large disc under its stomach and has to be considered as a distant relation of the Bull of Guisando. On the other side of the square, the former Lezama Railway Station is now the site of the new **Biscay Archaeology Museum**, created to tell the tale of the province's rich past through its wealth of archaeological remains and to promote research. Ideally, visitors should tour both museums in order to obtain a full insight into the history of this land.

The **Plaza de Unamuno** has a bust of the writer, the entrance to the Metro and the start of the **Calzadas de Mallona** (Mallona Steps) which linked the town with the Anteiglesia de Begoña (Parish of Begoña). The stairs lead to the **basilica**, gothic in style and built in 1519. It is also possible, and more comfortable, to go up to Begoña using the lift located in calle Esperanza behind the church of San Nicolás. The basilica's main doorway is plateresque and both the basilica and the Virgin to which it is dedicated are much loved and revered by the people of Vizcaya.

Below, a bust of Miguel de Unamuno, standing in the square of the same name.

Above, the archway leading into Mallona Cemetery.
Below, the exterior of the Biscay Archaeological Museum.

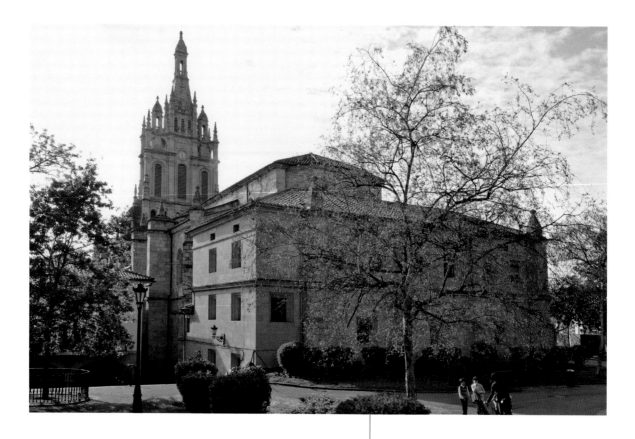

Above, view of the Basilica of Begoña.

At number 7 calle de La Cruz, next to plaza de Unamuno is where the writer lived as a child and in the house opposite, number 6, is where José Antonio de Aguirre y Lekube, the first lehendakari (Basque President) of the Basque Government, was born.

Plaza Nueva is a few metres away, similar to other arcades such as the Plaza Mayor in Madrid or Salamanca. Designed in the 18th century and completed a century later, it soon became the recreational centre of the town. One of its buildings acts as the headquarters of **Euskaltzaindia**, the Academy of the Basque Language and its porticos are used to hold the Sunday market of books, stamps, birds, etc. and an array of activities during the august celebrations known as Aste Nagusia. It is a stopping place for those who wish to sample the typical pintxos (elaborate tapas) or relax on a terrace. One of the entrances leads to the **church of Saint Nicolás** which was a fishermen's chapel in the middle ages. In 1754, Ignacio Ibero took charge of the construction of a house of God, the original floor plan of which was octagonal. Inside there are five magnificent altarpieces by the sculptor Juan de Mena. The facade,

Next page, the Church of San Nicolás.

Previous double page, the relaxed street café atmosphere in Plaza Nueva.

Below, panoramic view of the tidal estuary and Bilbao City Hall.

Above, Bilbao's new City Hall.

next to the entrance, bears a commemorative plaque indicating the level reached by the floods of 1983. Next to the church is the palacio **Gómez de la Torre**, a neoclassic palace dating back to the end of the 18th century, and at the rear in calle Esperanza, is the aforementioned lift which goes as far as Begoña.

In front of the church of Saint Nicolás are gardens called **El Arenal**, which stretch from the **Arriaga Theatre** to the **Town Hall of Bilbao**. These gardens used to be a beach, hence their name (El Arenal, The Sandy Area), then quay and from the 18th century a place for recreation, shaded with acacias and lime trees. On Sundays a flower market is held in **El Arenal** and a modernist concert is given by the Municipal Band on the kiosko (bandstand). On one Saturday of each month, it is also customary to have a display of traditional

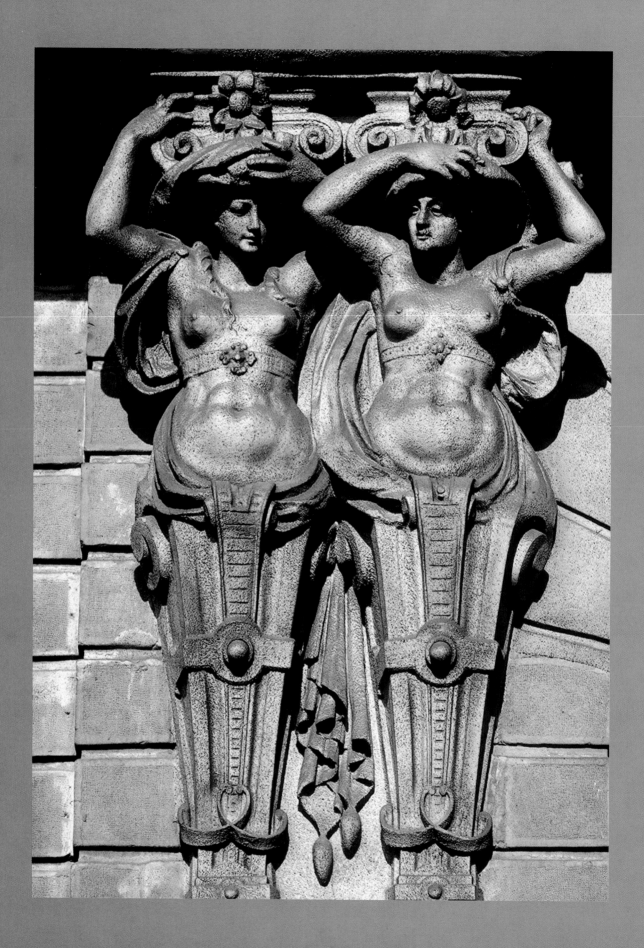

Basque dances in which anyone who wishes can participate. During the summer fiestas, El Arenal is full of txosnas, the popular marquees with music.

The **Arriaga Theatre** was built in 1890 and is named after the local composer Juan Crisóstomo de Arriaga, who died aged 19 and who was, nevertheless, considered "the Spanish Mozart" at the beginning of the 19th century. The building is the work of Joaquín Rucoba, who also built the **Casa Consistorial** (Town Hall) and reminiscent of the Paris Opera House. It is spectacular inside. Like almost all of the old quarter, it was renovated after the recent floods and is now firmly consolidated as a major multicultural

Previous page, atlantes on the side façade of the Arriaga Theatre.
Below, a close up of the back of the building.

Next double page, a view of the Arriaga Theatre by night.

space: it draws the finest dance and theatre companies as well as hosting numerous concerts, film festivals and other social events. Rehabilitation work has also recently been carried out on the **Boulevard Café**, one of Bilbao's classic venues, which stands just across the road from the theatre. When threatened with closure, hundreds of the city's residents rallied to prevent its disappearance.

Two roads which are vital for local business end at **El Arenal**: the streets known as Bidebarrieta and Correo. These form part of the

A panoramic view of Bilbao from Etxebarria Park.

A coat-of-arms on the corner of the Allendesalazar Palace façade.

old zone which grew outside the town walls and in the former there are impressive palaces worth mentioning such as the **Mazarredo Palace**, which is adorned with a huge coat of arms. This is the street where the **Municipal Library** can be found, designed by the architect Severino de Achúcarro. It was built at the end of the 19th century to accommodate the headquarters of the **Society El Sitio** which commemorates the blockade suffered by the town during the last Carlista War. It is one of Bilbao's most important cultural centres. The calle Correo links **El Arenal** and the **cathedral of Santiago**. Other sights worthy of mention on the same street are the neoclassic **Gortázar Palace** and the baroque **Allendesalazar Palace**.

Very close, stands the **palacio de los Vargas**, (Palace of the Vargas Family) which dates back to the 17th century. It is located in the calle de La Torre and now houses the **Stock Exchange.** Opposite the entrance, a mark on the ground indicates the exact place from where the **Begoña Basilica** can be seen in the distance. It is also worth stopping at the **fuente del Perro** from 1800, in the neighbouring calle del Perro. This fountain is neoclassic in style and its name, which was eventually given to the entire street, is the source of legendary confusion: the heads over which the water flows are not dogs but lions.

Close up of the front of the Stock Exchange.

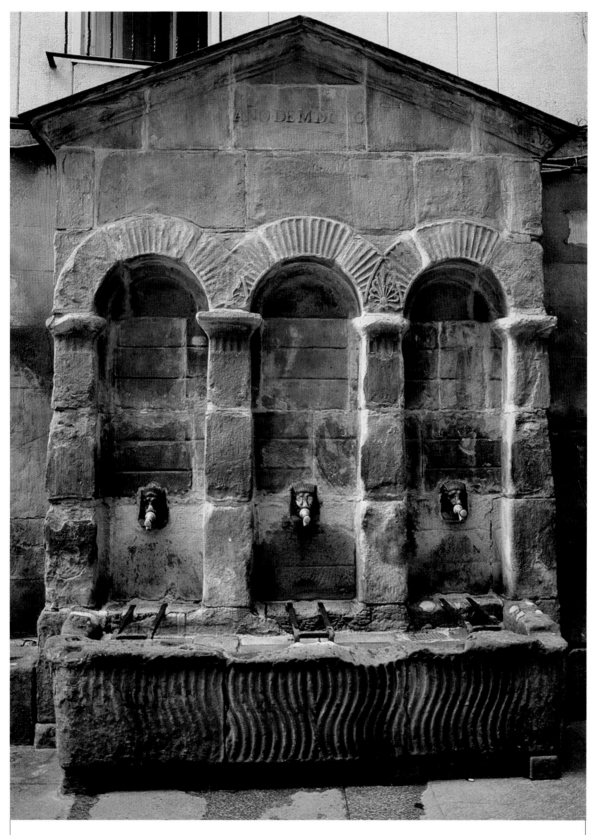

The much-loved Dog Fountain in Old Bilbao.

This page, two views of the Municipal Library. Left, a close up of the stained glass windows; below, the auditorium.

El Arenal Bridge links Old Bilbao
with the new town, known as El Ensanche.

THE NEW BILBAO – EL ENSANCHE

The population of Bilbao grew constantly from its founding up to the end of the 19th century, point in time when an extremely sharp increase began. In 1880 it had 11,000 inhabitants and only two decades later this figure had multiplied by seven. Workers from all over Spain immigrated, drawn by the economic development of Bilbao and its surroundings, and in a very short space of time there was a dramatic change in the social and urban physiognomy. It was an era characterised by momentous historical events such as the *Zamacolada* (a popular revolt against forced conscription into the king's troops) the occupation of the town by Napoleonic troops and, above all, the Carlista Wars. Bilbao suffered various blockades and since then is renowned for being a liberal town. The Estuary adapted itself to circumstances: the company **Ferrocarril Bilbao–Tudela** (Bilbao- Tudela Railway) was founded in 1857. **The Banco de Bilbao** (Bank of Bilbao) was created in the same year, in 1882 the steel foundry **Altos Hornos** and in 1891 the commodities exchange was put into operation. One year later the **Town Hall** was inaugurated and in 1897 the **Escuela de Ingenieros** (College of Engineers) opened.
All of the above made the enlargement of the town towards the other side of the river Nervión essential. The Seven Streets and the surroundings were not sufficient to respond to new demands. In

The FEVE or Santander Railway Station.

1876, the El Ensanche project was approved in which the following architects participated: Severino de Achúcarro, Ernesto Hoffmeyer and Pablo de Alzola. At the beginning of the 20th century, Bilbao ceased to be a dark labyrinth of intertwining narrow streets and spread out towards the areas of Abando, Begoña, Deusto and even Erandio. From the Seven Streets the other side of the Estuary is reached by crossing the **puente del Arenal**. After the floods, referred to as the aguaduchus, the Carlista Wars and the Civil War, little was left of the first bridge, christened with the name of Isabel II in 1845. It had a bascule section that could be raised and lowered to allow ships to pass. Immediately after crossing the bridge on the left is the Railway Station, the popular **Tren de La Robla** (Robla Train), which was of paramount importance for the economic and demographic growth of the town. A little further ahead are the headquarters of the **Sociedad Bilbaína**, a bourgeois club copied from the English clubs. Its members usually met in plaza Nueva, however in 1913 they decided to move to

This artistic stained glass window, which presides over the platforms of the Abando-Indalecio Prieto or North Station, tells the history of the city.

Monument to Diego López de Haro.

Plaza Circular seen.

the other side of the Estuary. The building was designed by the architect Emiliano Amann and is Viennese in style. Its interior is outstanding for its magnificence. It boasts a splendid library and a wonderful collection of Basque paintings.

The **Official Commodities Exchange** stands right next to the Sociedad Bilbaína. There used to be stockbrokers in the Boulevard, the Arriaga, plaza Nueva and in the Banco de Bilbao de San Nicolás, however with the new century they also turned their attention to the other side of the Nervión. In 1905 they inaugurated their own headquarters behind the **Estación del Norte** (North Station), also referred to as the **Estación de Abando-Indalecio Prieto**. This was where the first fixed Bilbao bullring was, apart from the one which used to be erected in days gone by next to Saint Antón. The current bullring, plaza de Vista Alegre, was inaugurated in 1882 and, after suffering a severe fire, rebuilt in 1962.

Continuing upwards takes the visitor to the Plaza Circular, the starting point for the main avenues of El Ensanche. On one side is **Abando-Indalecio Prieto Station**, a vital communications link and the station for the future high speed trains. This is a hub for commuter and long distance lines, and also has a metro station that connects the centre with the outlying districts and the municipalities of **Greater Bilbao**.

Next page, top, Plaza Circular seen from Gran Vía; below, inside the Bilbao metro.

Left, entrance to the metro station in Plaza Circular. These glass-fronted structures are known affectionately in the city as "fosteritos", as a tribute to their designer, Norman Foster.

There is also a tram stop very nearby. The station is overlooked by one of the highest and emblematic buildings, the BBV (Banco Bilbao Vizcaya). On the other side of the square is the **Café La Granja**, the place for gatherings, rendezvous and business meetings. **Plaza Circular** is overlooked from his pedestal by Diego López de Haro, the founder of the town who is seen holding the Town Charter in his right hand. This is the starting point of Bilbao's main avenue, the **Gran Vía**, in the heart of the new town. To the left and right are outstanding buildings which are proof of Bilbao's economic strength. It is worth strolling from the plaza Circular to the **plaza del Sagrado Corazón**, at the other end of Gran Vía, to enjoy the elegant palaces, the majority of which are in the hands of public

Albia Gardens.

institutions. The first urbanised square of El Ensanche was los **jardines de Albia**, a few metres away from the Gran Vía. Today these gardens represent a small, tree-lined oasis in the middle of buzzing business. They have the statues of Antonio de Trueba, Antón el de los Cantares, and Sabino Arana. The first was a costumbrismo writer during the 19th century and the second founder of the PNV, the Basque Nationalist Party. The house of his birth was nearby, however was demolished and the same ground was used to build Sabin Etxea, the PNV's headquarters. This is also the location of the **Palacio**

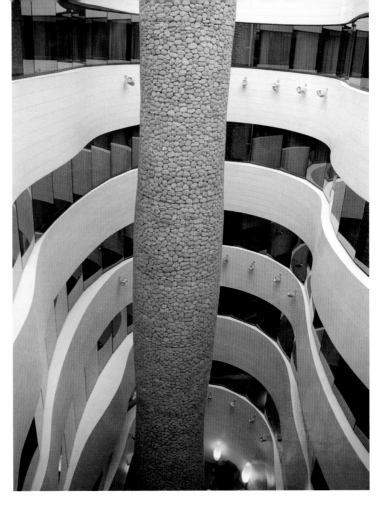

*Right, inside the Hotel Domine,
designed by J. Mariscal.
Below, shops lining Gran Vía.*

de Justicia (Lawcourts) and **San Vicente Mártir**, the old parish of the Anteiglesia de Abando. It was founded in 1190, rebuilt during the 16th century and reformed during the 19th century. Its side doorway is gothic from the 14th century. It has three naves, and Antonio Trueba is buried here in a tomb in the wall.

Next to San Vicente is one of the town's most representative entertainment venues, the **Kafe Antzokia**. Inaugurated in 1995 with the intention of promoting Basque culture, it organises hundreds of concerts of all types. It is also one of the most visited venues during festivals or at night by bilbaínos. On the other side of the Albia Gardens is the **Iruña**, a traditional café and restaurant "since time immemorial". Going back to the **Gran Vía**, the visitor crosses calle Ledesma, another typical venue for chiquiteo. Walking to plaza del **Sagrado Corazón**, there is an abundance of splendid buildings such as the old **Banco de Bilbao**, the **palacio de la Diputación Foral** (Regional Council Offices) and in the **plaza Elíptica**, or **plaza Moyúa**, stands the **palacio de Chávarri** (Chávarri Palace), the headquarters of the Civil Government. The **Carlton Hotel** is also in this square which, during the 1936 Civil War, gave

Previous page, above, a monument in honour of Antonio Trueba; below, inside the Iruña café and restaurant.

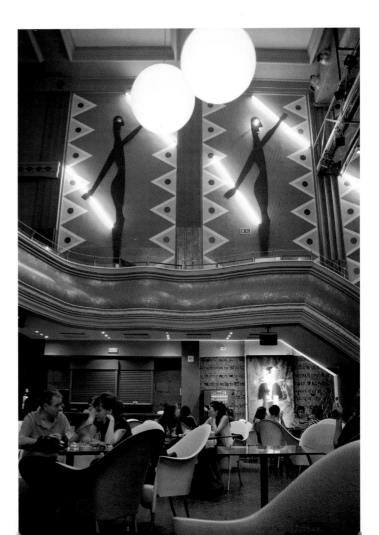

Right, inside the Kafe Antzokia.

shelter to the Basque Government presided over by the Lehendakari Aguirre.

Standing in the centre of the square and looking into the distance, in any direction, it is obvious why Bilbao is referred to as El Botxo (the hole): it is an urban conglomeration surrounded by hills, almost squeezed in between them. Seven hills surround and protect it. The most popular of these is Artxanda. The easiest and most attractive way of getting to the top of Artxanda is using the funicular railway which gradually reveals the town during its ascent.

The façade of Casa Montero.

Previous page, and this page, above, two views of the square known as Plaza Elíptica or Moyúa.

La Huella *(The Fingerprint)*, a sculpture by Juan José Novella that stands in Artxanda.

Once at the top, you can delight in a panoramic view of Bilbao and its surroundings. Many bilbaínos visit it at the weekends to stroll, eat or enjoy the views, which stretch out as far as the sea. It is also a popular spot with newly-weds who choose to have their wedding photographs taken here. It is also the site of La Huella ('The Fingerprint'), a sculpture in carbon steel by Juan José Novella which was inaugurated in 2006. Standing six metres in height and weighing almost eight tons, it pays tribute to the militia and gudaris that defended Bilbao during the Civil War. Once a year, several public institutions and local associations organise a march to this spot to honour the memory of those that fought against Franco's regime.

A few metres from Moyúa Square is the **parque de Doña Casilda**. For a long time it was the main, and almost only, green oasis in the town until other huge parks were created such as **parque de Europa** in Txurdinaga, **parque de La Peña** or **parque de Etxebarria** located between the Seven Streets and Begoña. This clear commitment to improving the quality of life of its inhabitants is one of the most marked changes to affect the new Bilbao. In 2002 a private study qualified its "green urban area" as the best equipped in Spain with regard to cleaning services, accesses, bicycle lanes, sport areas, swings etc. In this regard, the parque de Doña Casilda, which today is still known as El Parque without having to use it full name, was very much on its own in the past. It is a place for recreation and relaxation with ponds, sculptures, secluded corners, silent strolls and a play area for children. La Pérgola in the park is used as a venue for various concerts during the august festivities. It is also

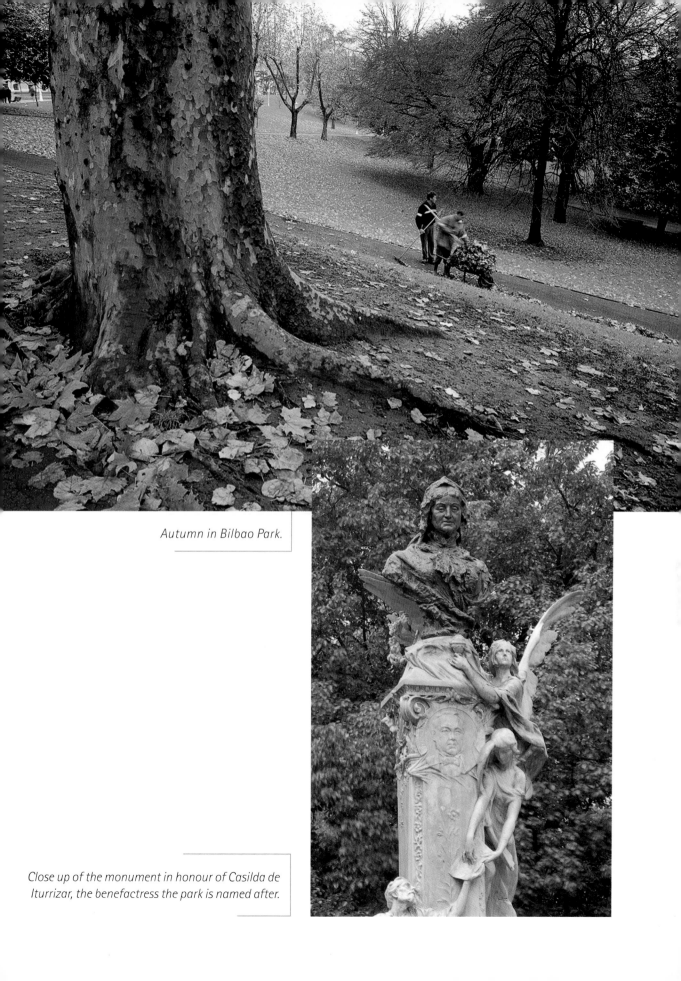

Autumn in Bilbao Park.

Close up of the monument in honour of Casilda de Iturrizar, the benefactress the park is named after.

An exterior view of the Fine Arts Museum.

home to the recently reformed **Museum of Fine Arts** which has experienced an exceptional rise in interest thanks to the arrival of tourists drawn initially to the **Guggenheim Museum.**

Bilbao's Museum of Fine Arts has been the town's hidden jewel for many decades and owes its foundation in 1914 to the initiative of the Diputación de Vizcaya (Government of Vizcaya), the Ayuntamiento de Bilbao (Bilbao Council) and various other local collectors. It was created during a period of social and cultural modernisation with the intention of giving the artistic community exemplary models for their training. It was supervised by the painter Manuel Losada and, initially, was set up in the Escuela de Artes y Oficios in **Atxuri** near the Seven Streets. He soon began to receive generous donations and bequests from institutions and private individuals and, a decade later, his success encouraged the creation of a second museum dedicated to contemporary art. This **Museo de Arte Moderno**, located in offices belonging to the Council, was supervised by the painter Aurelio Arteta. Once the Civil War had come to an end it was decided to design a new area to unite the collections of both museums in the new part of the town. Neoclassic in style, according to the project of the architects Fernando Urrutia and Gonzalo Cárdenas, the building was inaugurated in 1945 and declared a Monument of Historical-Artistic Importance in 1962. After various remodelling measures and enlargements, in 1991 the Basque Government entered to form part of the Museum and, under the management of Miguel Zugaza, a magnificent transformation took place which led to it being reinaugurated in 2001. It is home to one of the best art galleries in Spain and is a must for anyone wishing to delight in Basque painting. Its permanent collection includes works by Diego de la Cruz, El Greco, Anton Van Dyck, Martin de Vos, Bartolomé Esteban Murillo, Francisco de Zurbarán, Francisco de Goya, Paul Gauguin, Paul Cézanne, Darío de Regoyos, Ignacio Zuloaga, Joaquín Sorolla, José Gutiérrez Solana, Aurelio Arteta, Jorge Oteiza, Eduardo Chillida, Antoni Tàpies, etc. Its temporary exhibitions are also superb.

The Fine Arts Museum: right, a sculpture dedicated to the musician Juan Crisóstomo de Arriaga, the so-called 'Muse of Arriaga'; below, the entrance to the museum.

BILBAO IN THE 21ST CENTURY

In 1988, renowned Bilbao-born journalist Luis del Olmo entitled one of his books *Bilbao, cómo has cambiao* (Bilbao, how you've changed). Nobody could have imagined what was to come, the magnificent transformation which is the pride of its inhabitants and astonishing to visitors. In honour of a known saying, Bilbao was strong in the face of adversity and took advantage of two disasters which occurred during the last quarter of the 20th century to bring out its best: on the one hand, the terrible floods gave impetus to the renovation of the most damaged part of the town, the Seven Streets and the surrounding area. On the other hand, the industrial restructuring made the town reinvent itself both on an urban and social level. Many bilbaínos initially viewed the institutional challenge with mistrust and incredulity. Projects such as the Metro and the Guggenheim Museum sparked great controversy and only their indisputable success has put an end to the majority of the criticisms. Bilbao immediately began to fill with tourists and prominent visitors who were accompanied by many international hotel chains, luxury restaurants, upmarket clothes and accessories shops, etc. Thus the change in the town's appearance also led to a change of mentality in its inhabitants. Initial discouragement and indifference has given way to a healthy and stimulating pride. Although there is still a quite melancholic feeling with regard to that grey Bilbao of bygone years, almost no one feels a real desire to go back to these times anymore.

Out of necessity the port area, **Abandoibarra**, was restructured and turned into an area for recreation, leisure and services. In the space of a few years, various hotels, shopping centres, play areas for children and three bridges: **Euskalduna**, **Pasarela del Padre Arrupe** and **Zubi–zuri** by Santiago Calatrava have been built along the Estuary as well as a magnificent promenade along the

Below, Euskalduna Bridge; right, the Padre Arrupe Footbridge.

*Previous double
page, Zubi-zuri
Bridge and the
Isozaki Atea.*

*Left, the
headquarters
of the Osakidetza
- the Basque Health
Service.*

Nervión. This area, from Olabeaga to El Arenal, can be visited on foot or from the tram, another of the recent developments incorporated into Bilbao's landscape. The local skyline has also changed considerably in recent years with the construction of the magnificent buildings that make up the Isozaki Atea complex, designed by Japanese architect Arata Isozaki with the collaboration of local city architect Iñaki Aurrekoetxea. The highlights of this complex are two imposing glass-fronted towers that house luxury apartments. The most recent addition to this cityscape is the Iberdrola Tower, completed in 2012. This business centre and office block is the work of Argentinean architect Cesar Pelli. With a height of 165 metres and 41 floors, it holds the title of the tallest skyscraper in the

Above, the Iberdrola Tower.

*Above left,
the new University
of Deusto
library building.*

Basque Country and indeed the entire Cantabrian coast.

Abandoibarra's central esplanade is the site of a superb cultural triangle: on one side we find the **Guggenheim Museum**, described in greater detail later on; on the second side the **Learning and Research Resource Centre**, also known as the new library of the **University of Deusto**, designed by the architect Rafael Moneo and which opened in 2009; and on the third and final side, the **Auditorium of the University of the Basque Country**, the work of architect Álvaro Siza and which opened in 2010.

Two important buildings, flanking each side of the **Museum of Fine Arts**, represent the pinnacle of this

revolutionary change: the Palacio Euskalduna and the Guggenheim Museum. The **Palacio Euskalduna de Congresos y de la Música**, a congress centre and auditorium, is located at the west end of the parque de Doña Casilda. It symbolises the last ship built in the shipyard and was designed by the architects Federico Soriano and Dolores Palacios. It was inaugurated in 1999, has various areas and hosts a multitude of activities. Its artistic programme includes dance, theatre, opera and modern music events. In 2003 it was given an award for the best Congress Centre in the world.

The **Guggenheim Museum** is the flagship of Bilbao's transformation. The process for its construction started in 1991. Two years later the foundation stone was laid and in 1997 the impressive building designed by Frank O. Gehry was inaugurated. Puppy, an enormous floral dog by Jeff Koons, welcomes visitors to the museum. According to a local joke, which is telling with regard to the character of the Bilbainos, the museum is merely the kennel for this appealing pooch. Behind the museum, along the

Left, the auditorium of the University of the Basque Country;
below, close up of the exterior of the Euskalduna Convention Centre.

Above, Puppy stands guard over the Guggenheim.

promenade, pedestrians can walk under the legs of the bronze Mamá, from the Araña (Spider) series by Louise Bourgeois. It is also considerable in size. The building is made of a series of interconnected volumes, clad in limestone with titanium sheathing. Added to this is glass, curvilinear and twisted shapes, and the overall effect is breathtaking. Depending on the time of day, light is reflected differently on its structures and the museum itself, gigantic, is fully reflected on the water of the Nervión. If possible, it is also worth seeing it at night, from the Deusto Bridge.

Its spectacular interior consists of 19 galleries. One of these is 130 metres long and 30 metres wide, without columns, the ideal exhibition room for works of art which would otherwise be difficult to fit into the usual rooms. Its collection and exhibitions attract thousands of

Right, Mamá, a sculpture by Louise Bourgeois, situated outside the Guggenheim Museum.

visitors and the museum adds lustre to the daily life of Bilbainos since it is used for presentations and various social events.

Very few visitors to the museum are aware that just five days prior to its official opening the *Ertzaintza*, the Basque Country's autonomous police force, prevented a terrorist attack by ETA planned for the opening day. An officer spotted two men acting suspiciously in the area around the museum. When asked to provide some form of ID, one of the men drew out a gun and shot the officer dead. It is for this reason that the square leading to the museum is known as Plaza de José María Aguirre – the name of the murdered police officer.

By walking from the Guggenheim Museum towards the coast, the visitor quickly comes across **Bilbao's Maritime Museum** (Museo Marítimo Ría de Bilbao), another of the town's innovations. It was inaugurated at the end of 2003 and is built upon an immense area which accommodated the docks for the Euskalduna shipyards prior to the restructuring. The **Carola Crane**, commemorates and symbolises a non-too-distant past. The history of this crane, which was erected in 1957, is well worth telling. The story goes that when the shipyards were fully operational, many women would take their husbands' lunch across the river by boat. One of them was so beautiful that the workers would climb the crane to admire her and call out compliments. The woman's name was Carola, and so the crane became known by the same name. An alternative version of the tale is that she was really a secretary at Deusto who would walk to her office everyday along the riverside.

Above and on the previous page, various views of the Guggenheim Museum.

The Abandoibarra riverside walk and the Guggenheim Museum.

This double page, two panoramic views of the Ría de Bilbao Maritime Museum.

The interior of the Maritime Museum is divided into three major areas: The Nervión and its banks as a maritime port, as a market and factory and as a naval shipyard. It provides information regarding both the physical changes in the area as well as the social and cultural changes driven by the economic activity in the Estuary.

Nevertheless, the New part of Bilbao comprises much more than the rehabilitated area of Abandoibarra. In addition to the creation of neighbourhoods such as Miribilla, the revitalisation of Ametzola, the pedestrianisation of some streets in the centre and the gradual regeneration of the Old Bilbao, is the idea of a complete remodelling of the Zorrotzaurre peninsula. The anglian-Iraqian architect Zaha Hadid has been enlisted for this task. Set against this ongoing backdrop of renewal and improvement work, we find the new, up-and-

Previous page. Above, Ametzola, one of Bilbao's new residential districts built on the site of a former freight station. Above, a game of pelota vasca being played on the new Bizkaia frontón.

coming district known as Miribilla, famed for its outstanding sports facilities. It boasts the highly original recently-built Bilbao Arena Sports Centre, home to the Bizkaia Bilbao basketball team, with a capacity for 8,500 spectators, and also the Bizkaia fronton, the largest in the Basque Country and for many years a deeply-cherished ambition of many local fans of *pelota vasca*. "About time too", were the words of city mayor Iñaki Azkuna at the opening ceremony, aptly summing up the feelings of many of the city's residents.

Previous page, below, an exterior view of the Bilbao Arena Sports Centre; left, a basketball match being played inside the Centre.

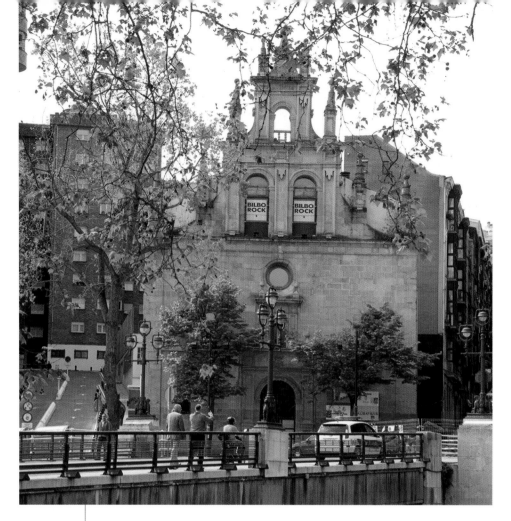

Bilborock, and the ancient Church of La Merced,
the venue for recent editions of the City of Bilbao Pop-Rock Contest.

LEISURE AND CULTURE

One of the most outstanding characteristics of 21st century Bilbao is its strong thrust as a cultural and leisure capital. In addition to the well-known **Guggenheim** and **Fine Arts Museums**, there are others such as the **Maritime**, **Taurine** and **Basque Museums** as well as that of **Reproducciones Artísticas** (Artistic Reproductions) and several art galleries and exhibition halls.

As far as music is concerned, the concerts organised by **ABAO, The Bilbao Association of Friends of Opera** are the most outstanding. More avid rock fans will enjoy those organised against very original backdrops such as **Azkena**, **Kafe Antzokia, Fever** and **Bilborock**. The latter is a convent converted into a multipurpose hall and in which the **Concurso Pop–Rock Villa de Bilbao** is held, the most interesting of its kind in Spain. Lovers of jazz, and other more daring styles, must not miss the **Bilbaína Jazz Club** programme. It is also worth highlighting the increased theatre variety both in the large scenarios of the **Arriaga Theatre, Campos Theatre** or the **Euskalduna Palace** as well as smaller and more alternative ones such as **La Fundición** (The Foundry), **Arteria** and **Pabellón 6**.

The latest public contribution to culture and leisure in the city is the recently reformed **Alhóndiga** building. Built in the Modernist style and declared an "Asset of Cultural Interest" by the Basque Government in 1999, its 43,000 square metres play host to a wealth of activities. The various spaces

Above, Arteria; *below,* Pabellón 6, *alternative leisure venues in Zorrotzaurre.*

Above, the swimming pool at the Alhóndiga complex.

Previous page, above, view inside the Alhóndiga complex, and the terrace.

include a swimming pool, fitness room, exhibition hall, film and media libraries, auditorium and restaurant. Designed a century ago by local architect Ricardo Bastida, for years it was the object of heated debate between the local corporations and the opposition parties. Numerous proposals were put forward to give this former wine warehouse a new lease of life, including the construction of a sports centre, museum, apartment block and even a spectacular glass cube, an idea partially attributable to the sculptor Jorge Oteiza. The decision was eventually made to create a multipurpose space for cultural activities. French designer Philippe Starck was commissioned to carry out the extensive alteration work in the interior of this building, which retains much of the façade and structure of the original building.

Along these lines, the effort made by **BAD**, the festival of dance and theatre, is worthy of mention. Events such as the **Feria del Libro de Ocasión** (Opportunity Book Fair) and the **Festival de Cine Documental y Cortometraje** (Festival of Documental and Short Film Cinema) can be added to this list as well as others which lend a cultural flavour to the traditional business role of the town. All of the above has led to the inauguration of various hotels and catering and leisure establishments and shops with a markedly avant-garde hallmark. The new wave of immigration, especially from Africa and Latin America, has increased the number of restaurants with an ethnic flavour and bazaars of imported products. The homosexual community is helping to liven the image of the town as being increasingly diverse. The **Zinegoak International Festival of Gay–Lesbian–Transexual Cinema** is proof of this.

The people of Bilbao, regardless of how, enjoy socialising on the streets. In spite of a climate which is not always favourable, groups of friends meet to have a drink or snack and to eat pintxos in areas such as Licenciado Poza, Ledesma or the Seven Streets. The renowned Basque Gastronomy can be sampled in restaurants of acclaimed cuisine, cider houses, grillrooms and at attractive bars in pubs. Occasionally, and especially during the fiestas, groups of men can be overheard singing bilbainadas, the local song par excellence. The town is at its most relaxed during the so-called Semana Grande of August (Great Week), **Aste Nagusia**, during which concerts, theatre, fireworks, rural Basque sporting shows, circus events and bullfights abound. During this period, Bilbao appears to congregate, ready to party, along both sides of the Arenal Bridge. The people of Bilbao also enjoy the fair of Santo Tomás, the day of San Blas, Santa Águeda, Carnival and other festivities of a religious kind such as Semana Santa (Easter), which is increasingly viewed as rating amongst Spain's most famous.

The Santa Águeda
Choir performing
in El Arenal.

The popular
Víctor Montes
Bar-Restaurant
in Plaza Nueva.

Previous page,
outdoor market in
Calle Dos de Mayo.
Right, traditional
Basque dances
during the Aste
Nagusia Festival.

However, if there is something which unites all the inhabitants of the town, beyond social class and ideological struggles it is Athletic de Bilbao, the local football team. The team is virtually unique in the world in that only players from the region are accepted. This characteristic swells the pride of fans in Vizcaya and that of thousands of followers who support the club outside the Basque Country. It is worth walking round the outside of **San Mamés**, the football stadium referred to as **The Cathedral**, to become immersed in the atmosphere or visiting when a match is being played. A truly unforgettable sight that visitors should make the effort to experience soon, as next to the old stadium work is already underway on San Mamés Barria, which is set to replace it and which has a capacity for 55,000 spectators. This new project is the result of heated debate and multiple projects and discussions between public organisation and the club's social mass.

Below left, Marijaia, the symbol of the Bilbao Festival; right, the fireworks contest.

Above, Athletic de Bilbao supporters; below, a Holy Week Procession and an exhibition of Basque country sports.

Finally, it must not be forgotten that the town is the centre of what is referred to as **Greater Bilbao** or, in its more ample and modern version, **Bilbao Metropolitano**. This group of thirty villages and towns is home to almost one million inhabitants, linked by a smooth network of communications and by many common objectives and projects. The transfer of the **International Trade Fair** from its old location next to San Mamés, to **Barakaldo**, has also witnessed the creation, in the industrial locality, of a huge number of shopping centres and department stores. Without having to stray far from Bilbao it is recommendable visiting some beautiful villages such as **Getxo**, with its marvellous marina, **Portugalete**, with the famous **Puente Colgante** (Suspension Bridge), also known as **Puente de Bizkaia**; **Gernika**, whose Casa de Juntas plays a crucial role in understanding the history of the Basque Country; or **Mundaka**, whose famous left-hand wave is renowned among surfers around the world. Other beaches such as **Sopelana**, **Muskiz**, **Plentzia** and **Bakio** are also all well worth a visit.

Right, shipyard cranes in Sestao, one of the tidal estuary's industrial hubs.
Below, the famous suspension bridge, known today as "Puente Bizkaia", which links both sides of the tidal estuary.

Double page, above, panoramic views of Greater Bilbao.

Below, the Bilbao Exhibition Centre in Barakaldo.

The stunning transformation of Vizcaya's capital has driven the development of the ring of municipalities that surround it and, in general, of the province and the entire Basque Country.

Above, Ereaga Beach with the port in the background.